THE GREAT BOOK OF ANIMAL KNOWLEDGE

KOMODO DRAGONS

Indonesian Land Crocodiles

Introduction

Have you ever heard stories about knights fighting a huge, fire-breathing dragon? Monstrous sized dragons with large wings that allow them to fly and destroy kingdoms? Today, the closest animal to that legendary creature is the komodo dragon. They can't fly, and don't spit fire, but the komodo dragons are amazing animals and deadly predators that can kill prey a lot bigger than themselves. They are the world's largest lizards, found only in Indonesia. Let's learn about the komodo dragon!

What Komodo Dragons Look Like

Photo by Tracy Hunter (flickr.com/tracyhunter), as licensed under CC BY 2.0 Generic

Komodo dragons have thick skin, a long tail, flat faces, and four short and bulky legs with sharp claws on it. They look quite similar to crocodiles. In fact, they are called Ora, or 'land crocodiles', by locals living near komodo dragons.

Size and Weight

Komodo dragons are the largest lizards in the world. They grow 10 ft (3 m) long! Weighing around 330 pounds (150 kg). Komodo dragons are also the heaviest species of lizard.

Senses

Photo by NAPARAZZI (flickr.com/naparazzi), as licensed under CC BY-SA 2.0 Generic

Komodo dragons have an excellent sense of smell. However, they don't actually use their nostrils to smell, they use their tongue! A komodo dragons tongue is forked like a snake's. When komodo dragons flick their tongue, they are actually picking up tiny scent particles. They put these scent particles in a special organ inside their mouth that helps them smell things.

What Komodo Dragons Eat

Photo by Molly Goossens (flickr.com/mollygoossens), as licensed under CC BY 2.0 Generic

Komodo dragons will eat any food they will find. Their main food, though, is deer. They also eat pigs, snakes, fish, and just about anything including baby and young komodo dragons! They even sometimes eat animals that are a lot bigger than them like water buffaloes!

Saliva

Komodo dragons have thick saliva full of bacteria. Scientists discovered 23 different types of bacteria in a komodo dragon's mouth! These bacteria are dangerous, and kill the victim of the komodo dragon's bite. This helps them kill prey that is too big for them to overpower.

Venom

Recent studies suggest that komodo dragons might actually be venomous animals. And that venom is actually the one that kills the komodo dragons' victims instead of the many bacteria on their saliva. There is no sure answer yet, though. More research still needs to be done for us to be sure.

Hunting

Komodo dragons are ambush hunters. They lie low, waiting for their prey to come nearby. Then they make a short burst to their prey and use their teeth and claws to hold on and kill it. If their prey luckily gets away, it will soon die because of the bacteria (or the venom). The komodo dragon will then find the dead body using it's tongue. Komodo dragons are dangerous hunters. They are even known to be capable of hunting humans.

Teeth

Komodo dragons have extremely sharp teeth that are perfect for tearing meat. Their teeth look similar to the teeth of a shark. And like sharks, komodo dragons also shed their teeth and grow newer, sharper ones. However, when a komodo dragon opens its mouth, you can't actually see their teeth. This is because the teeth are quite small, and they are covered by their gums.

Eating

Photo by Bob Jenkins (flickr.com/48380660@N04), as licensed under CC BY 2.0 Generic

When a komodo dragon eats, it doesn't chew its food because their teeth are not designed for chewing. Instead, komodo dragons swallow chunks of meat whole. They have powerful acids in their stomach that digest these chunks of meat. Komodo dragons don't have to eat every day. In fact, they can survive with only 12 meals a year! Komodo dragons make the most of the energy they get from their food.

Where Komodo Dragons Live

Komodo dragons can be found in islands of Indonesia, in Southeast Asia. They live in savannas, grasslands, and open woodlands. Wild komodo dragons can only be found in only 5 islands. 4 of these 5 islands are part of the Komodo National Park. This park was founded to protect the komodo dragons declining population.

Burrows

Some komodo dragons like to dig shallow burrows. They rest in these burrows during nighttime and during daytime when the sun is up and it's super hot. They also use old burrows made by other komodo dragons for shelter.

Swimming

Komodo dragons are very good swimmers. Sometimes, they swim between the 4 islands of the Komodo national park! They swim from island to island to find a mate or to hunt their favorite prey. Although they are good swimmers, komodo dragons rarely swim in the open sea.

Behavior

Komodo dragons are solitary animals, this means that they don't live in groups, they live alone. However, they often come together to share a big meal. This is one of the only times you can see komodo dragons together. They also come together to mate.

What Komodo Dragons Do

Photo by prilfish (flickr.com/silkebaron), as licensed under CC BY 2.0 Generic

Komodo dragons are diurnal animals. This means that they are mostly active during daytime. Komodo dragons wake up in the morning and warm themselves by staying under the sun. Then they go hunting! When the hottest time of the day arrives, komodo dragons will return to their burrow to rest. They leave their burrow again to look for food, or just walk around, and return to a burrow during nighttime to sleep.

Breeding

Female komodo dragons don't breed every year. They rest to regain the energy they lost during their egg production. Male komodo dragons use their tongues to know if a female is ready to mate. They sometimes have to fight with other males to have the right to mate. Female komodo dragons lay 15-30 eggs inside a nest on the hillside or ground. They also use mound nests build by orange-footed scrub fowls that are unoccupied.

Baby Komodo Dragons

After 8-9 months, the eggs hatch. The baby komodo dragons are instantly on their own when they hatch; the mother doesn't take care of them. They quickly climb up trees and live there to avoid being eaten by adult komodo dragons. While on the trees, young komodo dragons eat eggs, grasshoppers, birds, and geckos. Their prey gets bigger as they get bigger. Finally, when they are about 4 years old, young komodo dragons will try life on the ground.

Predators

Photo by Poppet Maulding (flickr.com/charmedhour), as licensed under CC BY 2.0 Generic

Adult komodo dragons are on top of the food chain. This means that they have no predators! However, young komodo dragons are sometimes killed and eaten by birds of prey and predatory mammals. Adults are one of the main threats to young komodo dragons. They see the young komodo dragons as easy meals!

Humans and Komodo Dragons

After their discovery during World War 1, komodo dragons have fascinated humans and made lots of people afraid of them. Many tourists visit the Komodo national park to see the king of lizards. However, there have been some bad relations between humans and komodo dragons. People used to hunt the komodo dragons for their teeth and skin. And komodo dragons are not friendly to humans. They attack and can kill humans!

Endangered

Photo by eileenmak (flickr.com/eileenmak), as licensed under CC BY 2.0 Generic

Sadly, despite being big, strong, and on top of the food chain, komodo dragons are now endangered. They are threatened by habitat destruction, illegal poaching, and natural disasters. There are only about 3000-5000 komodo dragons left in the wild. However, because of conservation efforts, the population of komodo dragons is rising!

Relatives

Photo by John Tann (flickr.com/31031835@N08), as licensed under CC BY 2.0 Generic

Komodo dragons are monitor lizards. Monitor lizards all have long necks, powerful tails, and strong claws. Most monitor lizards are carnivores, or meat-eaters, but there are some species that eat fruits. Other monitor lizards include the Bengal monitors, Nile monitors, goannas, and desert monitors.

Get the next book in this series!

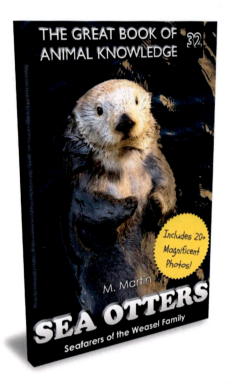

SEA OTTERS: Seafarers of the Weasel Family

Log on to Facebook.com/GazelleCB for more info

Tip: Use the key-phrase "The Great Book of Animal Knowledge" when searching for books in this series.

For more information about our books, discounts and updates, please Like us on FaceBook!

Facebook.com/GazelleCB

Made in the USA
Middletown, DE
19 November 2022

15533008R00018